From the Locker Room to the Classroom

BECOMING A CHAMPION *STUDENT*-ATHLETE

Professor Adonis "Sporty" Jeralds

DEDICATION

Dedicated to all the student athletes living their
dream of competing at the collegiate level. May you always
strive to be a CHAMPION on and off the field.

CONTENTS

ACKNOWLEDGMENTS

I would like to thank all my colleagues who share their knowledge and expertise with my students at the University of South Carolina in SPTE 490—The Student-Athlete Experience. Jeff Crane, John Dozier, Emily Epting, Jared Evans, Maria Hickman, Holly Johnson, John Kasik, Erin Kitchell, Brittany Lane, Theresa Logan, Dr. Mike McCall, Officer Jim Miles, Shannon Nix, Blake Taylor, Judy Van Horn, Charles Waddell and Dr. Carl Wells are all true professionals who care deeply about improving the lives of young people; Felicia Hall-Allen, Clint Bryant, Patrick Hairston, Judy Rose and John Thompson for their endorsement of this book; Anne Little, Josh Rosen, Minikki Stevens and Bryony Waddell for editing the book; Pierre Banks, Steve Joyner, Kylie Murphy, Duke Pryor, Jason Singleton, Randall Stewart, Greg Turner and Kim Whitestone for their support over the years; Andy Greenwell, Jack Jensen, Ike Walker, George Wallace and Otis Williamson for sharing their wisdom; and my family and friends for their support of all my projects. May God Bless You!

INTRODUCTION

Hello Student-Athlete,

Congratulations on your opportunity to compete in intercollegiate athletics. This booklet is designed to give you information that will allow you to have a successful career on and off the field of play.

Each topic selected for this booklet is relevant as you begin your career as a student-athlete. As a full-time clinical instructor in the Department of Sport and Entertainment Management at the University of South Carolina, I have had the opportunity to teach some elite athletes over the years. A few years ago our department, in conjunction with Carolina's athletic department, designed a course specifically for incoming freshmen and transfer student-athletes. The purpose of the course is to provide the athletes with information that will help them transition from either high school or another university.

This three-credit-hour course utilizes full-time university personnel, athletic department staff members and community partners as speakers. Each of these speakers is an expert in their subject area. Our student-athletes are able to gather valuable information and ask questions of these experts. Over the years, I have learned a tremendous amount about these subjects and I want to share that information with other student-athletes around the country.

This booklet is based on the information shared by those experts, as well as my observations and experiences as an instructor. My hope is that it will provide a guide for you to make good decisions and get your college career off to a great start both academically and athletically.

CHAMPIONS KNOW THEIR DESTINY

SELECTING THE RIGHT MAJOR

From the time they are four or five years old, young people are asked the question, "What do you want to be when you grow up?" Often the answer is consistent with the positive images they see in everyday life, such as policemen, firemen or teachers. As they mature, they realize there are many more careers available. One of the most important decisions a student has to make during his or her college career is deciding on a major. A major is a specialized course of study that will hopefully prepare the student for their work life after college.

As I speak with student-athletes, more than 80 percent of them believe they have a chance to compete at the professional level. Of course, they believe competing professionally will guarantee them a comfortable living making plenty of money. Reality provides a more realistic picture of what is likely to happen. Most research indicates that less than 5 percent of the athletes that receive a college scholarship end up playing their sport professionally. Based on this information, selecting the right major is critically important as students are much more likely to be working a real job after college.

The Princeton Review has identified some of the reasons for selecting a major. Here are two of the primary reasons.

1. **Finding your passion** – It is very difficult for young people to know what they want to do after college. Studies have shown that more than 40 percent of students will change their major at some point during their college career. Studies have also indicated that the average 32-year-old will have had seven jobs after finishing college. One way to identify your passion is to finish this sentence: "If I had all the money I ever needed, I would want to wake up each day and _____."

2.	**Money** – There are quite a few quotes related to money. My favorite is, "Money is not that important, but it is right up there with air." You can't really do too much without money. There are many careers that pay extremely well. Unfortunately, these careers might not match up with what you love to do.

Whatever reason you use to decide on your major, know that it is a foundation to build on. Many people end up working outside of the subject they majored in during college and are quite successful.

CHAMPIONS MAXIMIZE EVERY MINUTE

TIME MANAGEMENT

Someone once said, "Freedom is not free." One of the biggest challenges facing college freshmen is time management. Young people are often excited to have the freedom to make their own choices and not have to listen to mom or dad.

I am proud that I have two master's degrees. I do feel it is important to share that after my first year of college I had a 1.5 grade point average. My biggest challenge was dealing with the freedom college provided. I would hang out in the dorm with friends most of the day. Around 2 p.m., I would head to basketball practice, then make it to the dining hall just in time for an early evening dinner, spend a couple of hours in the game room and finally head back to the dorm for more hanging out and a little studying. **My priorities were misplaced.** I could not find the right balance between everything competing for my time.

The letter I received from the Dean's office that summer notified me that I was on academic probation. I began to prioritize my time with added focus on studying and ended up making A's and B's my final three years.

As a student-athlete, you have four major areas to prioritize your time around: classes, studying, socializing and your sport-related commitments (practices, games, travel, film sessions, etc.). The ability to leave your teammate's dorm room while everyone is playing video games to read chapter 3 of your American History textbook takes great discipline. One advantage you have over regular students is that you don't have much free time. Because you have to devote time to your sport throughout the academic year, you are automatically forced to prioritize your time.

The Constitution of the United States of America states that all men are created equal. Although we may all be created equal, we are not all born with the same opportunities for success. The one equalizer is that we all have 24 hours per day. Use your time wisely!

CHAMPIONSHIP POINTERS

If you don't have time to do it right,
when will you have time to do it over?
John Wooden

Until you value yourself, you won't value your time.
Until you value your time, you will not do anything with it.
M. Scott Peck

Friends are thieves of time.
Francis Bacon

Don't wait. The time will never be just right.
Napoleon Hill

CHAMPIONS STUDY HARD
SUCCESSFUL STUDY STRATEGIES

As a college professor, I have the opportunity to teach many different types of students. I understand these students bring different motivations to my classroom. Over the years I have come to find that successful students use the seven specific strategies below. Using these strategies will allow you to be successful as you begin your college classes.

1. **Read The Syllabus** – If you were offered a multi-year contract to play your sport professionally, you would hopefully read the contract thoroughly before signing it. Consider a syllabus to be a contract between you and your professor. I am sure you have heard throughout your life that you should read all contracts very carefully. Although your university may encourage professors to use a specific format, each professor's syllabus will be different. The syllabus will include such items as the contact information and office hours for your professor, the learning objectives and grading criteria for the class, and the potential assignments and exams along with their respective due dates. Over the years, your professor will have had encountered certain situations with other students. Therefore, the syllabus acts as a frequently asked questions document. Your professor will become very frustrated if you ask a question through email or by phone that is already answered in your syllabus. **So Read The Syllabus!**

> The world belongs to those who read.
> **Rick Holland**

2. **Get To Know Your Professor** – Depending on the college or university you attend, your classes could be considerably larger than your high school classes. Some introductory classes at larger universities could have more than 300 students. It is very difficult for your professors to get to know you on a personal level in such a large environment. Therefore, it is important that you get to know your professors outside of class. All professors are required to keep office hours. Visiting your professors during their office hours will prove to them that you are serious about their class. You will get to know your professors on a more personal level and they will get to know you as well. If you are confused about any of your professors' expectations, a visit to their office will help clear up those questions. Most professors will give you specific study strategies and recommendations on how to best succeed in their class when you visit their office. Even if you have one short question that you feel could be answered before or after class, take the time to visit your professors during their office hours. A short 10-minute visit with your professors could be the best investment of your time during the semester. **So Get To Know Your Professor!**

A professor takes a hand, opens a mind and touches a heart.

3. **Participate, Don't Spectate** – As an athlete, you are used to being in the game and not sitting on the bench. You should have the same desire in your classes. In order for your professors to get to know you on a personal level, it is important that you participate in the class discussion. Always come prepared to ask questions and offer comments on the particular topic for that class. One suggestion for increasing your level of participation is to sit at the front of the class. It is very difficult for you to be distracted by classmates and other things going on in class if you are sitting right in front of your professor. You will naturally be more inclined to participate in class up front and subliminally you will tell the professor that you are engaged and care about what he or she is teaching. **So Participate, Don't Spectate!**

4. **Attend Every Class** – As an athlete, you would not think of missing a team meeting or film session for fear of missing something important related to your upcoming game. Similarly, you should do everything in your power to attend every class. You will find that professors have different attendance policies. Some require that you attend every class, while others look at you as adults and feel you can determine whether or not you should be in class. In order to make sure you do not miss any content or specific instructions related to upcoming classes or assignments, it is important that you attend **EVERY** class. If you must miss class because of your athletic events, doctor appointments or other reasons, make sure you communicate to your professor in advance that you will not be in class. When you miss class, you miss content. **So Attend Every Class!**

5. **Take Good Notes** – As an athlete, you are used to preparing for an opponent. You must also prepare for your quizzes, tests and exams the same way. One of the best methods of preparation is taking good notes during class. Early in your college career, you may find it difficult to determine what is most important from a lecture, and it is very difficult for you to write down everything the professor says. Therefore, you must actively listen to your professor. Most professors will either openly or subtlety give you a clue as to what the most important points are during their lectures. Phrases like "one of the key elements" or "you will see this again" are tip-offs that what comes next most likely will be on the next exam. A key element to taking good notes in class is the preparation you do before class. By reading your textbook or other assigned material, you will be familiar with what the instructor is teaching that day. You will have a sense of what is important during the lecture because you have seen the material before. Another strategy for enhancing your notes is to find study partners. By comparing notes with study partners, you will have an idea of what others felt was important during the lecture. Just as you have become proficient in your chosen sport through practice, in order to become great at taking notes, you must practice it as well. **So Take Good Notes!**

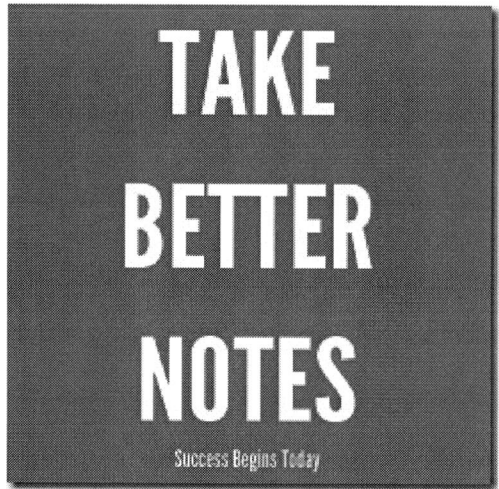

6. **Start Early** – The Top 10 Plays of the Day on ESPN often show a last-second buzzer-beater. Never would ESPN think of showing a 30-point blowout as part of their Plays of the Day, because, let's face it, a 30-point blowout is rather boring. I often hear students say that they do great under pressure and therefore they wait until the day before the exam or paper is due to begin studying or writing. In reality, what I have found is great students prepare early for exams and papers. They begin preparing early so they can reflect and make any necessary adjustments as they get closer to the exam or paper due date. A lot of times when we don't give ourselves enough time we make careless mistakes, forget details or allow unknowns such as computer viruses or an illness prevent us from doing our very best. Studying each day throughout the semester or having your term paper completed two weeks before it is due may be boring, but you will have a sense of accomplishment and more peace of mind if you keep up rather than trying to catch up. **So Start Early!**

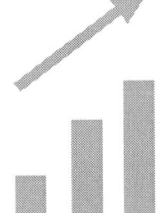

Start early and begin raising the bar throughout the day.

7. **Always Do The Extra Credit** – Just as you do extra work outside of practice to improve in your sport, it is important to do extra work to improve your academics. Most professors want you to do well and will offer extra credit at some point during a semester. You should always do the extra credit! While some students look at extra credit as optional, you should always believe extra credit assignments are mandatory. I have found in my classes that extra credit helps students get to another grade level or at least maintain their current grade. Good students will look at their grades and decide whether or not extra credit might help them improve their grade, but **great students always do the extra credit**. Extra credit opportunities happen at various times throughout the semester. Unfortunately, if you are struggling in a class, extra credit offered near the end of the semester may be too late to help you. **So Always Do The Extra Credit!**

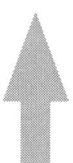

People of excellence go the extra mile

CHAMPIONS DON'T CHEAT

ACADEMIC INTEGRITY

Imagine walking into what appears to be a deserted locker room in the stadium before a championship game and finding one of your competitors taking a performance enhancing drug. Hopefully, you would immediately tell your coach and make sure that competitor was not allowed to play in the game. Athletes are conditioned to play hard but play fair. As far back as little league, we learn the rules of the game. We frown on those who take advantage of the rules to gain an advantage.

Similarly, not all college students play by the academic rules. There are several ways college students can gain an academic advantage over their fellow students. Gaining an academic advantage over other students falls under seven broad categories. Below are brief descriptions of those seven categories as outlined in the Honor Code at the University of South Carolina.

1. **Unauthorized Assistance** – Giving or receiving unauthorized assistance, or attempting to give or receive such assistance, in connection with the performance of academic work. Examples of unauthorized assistance include sharing of homework; cheating or allowing someone to cheat off an examination; or unauthorized collaboration such as working with another student on an assignment designed to be completed individually.

2. **Unauthorized Materials** – Unauthorized use of materials or information of any type, or unauthorized use of any electronic or mechanical device in connection with the completion of any academic work. Examples of unauthorized materials include using the textbook

during an online quiz although the syllabus prohibits it, use of a cell phone during an exam or taping equations on the back of a calculator.

3. **Lying** – Intentional misrepresentation by word or action of any situation or fact, or intentional omission of material fact so as to mislead any person in connection with any academic work. Examples of lying would include fabricating a doctor's note to delay taking an examination or signing in another student on the attendance sheet. **Remember, even a "little white lie" is a lie.**

4. **Unauthorized Access** – Unauthorized access to the contents of any test or examination, including the purchase, sale or theft of any test or examination prior to its administration. Examples of unauthorized access would include receiving a previous examination from an upperclassman or hacking into a professor's computer to find previous tests.

5. **Plagiarism** – Use of another person's work or ideas without proper acknowledgment of the source. Examples of plagiarism would include using a friend's paper when faced with a pressing deadline or using language from a 20-year-old magazine article and not giving credit to the original author.

6. **Bribery** – Offering or giving any favor or thing of value for the purpose of improperly influencing a grade or elevation of the student in an academic program. An example would include offering a professor complimentary tickets to a sold-out concert in exchange for a passing grade.

7. **Interference** – Conduct intended to interfere with an instructor's ability to evaluate a student's performance in an academic program. An example would be a student placing their name on a group project when they did none of the work.

Academic misconduct, academic fraud and academic dishonesty are all names we have heard for students gaining an academic advantage over their fellow students. **No matter the name, it is cheating.** It is important that you know the academic code of conduct for your college or university. Even if you unintentionally break the rules, you will be held accountable for your actions. If you ever have questions related to whether or not an action is inappropriate, be sure to refer to the syllabus or ask your instructor.

CHAMPIONSHIP POINTERS

Integrity is doing the right thing,
even when no one is watching.
C.S. Lewis

It is true that integrity alone will not make you a leader, but without
it you will never be one.
Zig Ziglar

If you have integrity nothing else matters, if you don't have integrity
nothing else matters.
Alan Simpson

Rather fail with honor than succeed by fraud.
Sophocles

EAT LIKE A CHAMPION

FUELING PEAK PERFORMANCE

Imagine you owned a thoroughbred horse that was capable of winning the Kentucky Derby. Hopefully, you would not feed him sugary cereal for breakfast, chili cheese fries for lunch and an all-you-can-eat buffet that included fried chicken for dinner. Similarly, if you owned a high-performance automobile such as a Lamborghini, you would not put regular fuel in the gasoline tank. You would definitely need high-octane fuel for your automobile to operate at its peak performance.

If you expect to operate at peak levels in your chosen sport, as well as academically, you need to fuel your body properly. One of the biggest challenges students entering college face is the freedom that allows you to eat whatever you want without mom or dad looking over your shoulders. For a lot of student-athletes who have performed at a very high level athletically during high school, the concept of proper nutrition has never crossed their mind. Because they have been very successful while eating whatever they want, they don't realize the different level their body could reach with the proper fuel. LeBron James is just one championship-level athlete who understands the importance of his nutrition and uses a personal chef. He understands proper nutrition has to be an integral part of his overall training regimen.

Below are five nutrition tips for athletes provided by WebMD.

1. **Load Up On Carbohydrates** – Carbs are an athlete's main fuel.

   - Your diet should get about 70 percent of its calories from carbohydrates such as bread, cereals, pasta, fruit and vegetables.
   - Avoid eating sugary or starchy foods within 30 minutes of practice or games as they can speed up dehydration.

- Replenish carbs and water during long workout sessions.

2. **Get Enough Protein, But Not Too Much** – Protein does not provide a lot of fuel for energy, but it is needed to maintain an athlete's muscles.

   - Getting too much protein can put a strain on your kidneys. Instead of protein supplements, eat high-quality protein such as lean meats, fish, chicken, turkey, nuts, beans, eggs or milk.
   - Drink Up. Joy Dubost, a registered dietician, says, "Milk is one of the best foods for recovery after an event because it provides a good balance of protein and carbohydrates." Milk also contains calcium, which contributes to strong bones.

3. **Go Easy On Fats** – Fats are contained in many of the foods normally consumed.

   - Most athletes get all the fat they need from foods such as nuts, avocados or fatty fish like salmon or tuna.
   - Avoid fatty foods on game day, as they may upset your stomach.

4. **Drink Fluids Early And Often** – Intense exercise, especially in hot weather, can quickly leave athletes dehydrated. Dehydration, in turn, can hurt your performance.

   - Athletes should drink early and often. If you wait until you are thirsty you are probably already dehydrated.
   - Because athletes lose fluids quickly, it is a good idea to drink plenty of fluids both before and during the event.

5. **Stay Away From Junk Food** – The food of today is different than the food eaten by our grandparents. Here are a few guidelines:

- Read food labels; stay away from chemicals.
- The closer to nature your food is, the better.
- The fewer hands that touched your food, the better.
- If it was made in a lab, it is off limits.
- If you can kill it or pluck it from the ground, it is fair game.

These tips are designed as guidelines for all athletes. It is important to note that each individual is different. Every athlete's metabolism and body composition are different. Different sports require different training regimens, which could require more or less food, as well as different types of food. Therefore, your nutritional plan has to be designed to meet your personal needs. You are responsible for what goes in your body. Do your own research, talk with professional dieticians and make informed choices.

CHAMPIONSHIP POINTERS

An apple a day keeps the doctor away.
Proverb

If you can't pronounce it, don't eat it.
Common Sense

To eat is a necessity, but to eat intelligently is an art.
La Rochefoucauld

Bigger snacks mean bigger slacks.
Author Unknown

CHAMPIONS GET PLENTY OF REST

A natural extension of placing the right kinds of foods in your body is to make sure you get the proper amount of sleep to operate at peak performance levels. Again one of the biggest temptations for students entering college is not having mom or dad stop by your bedroom and tell you to get off your phone or turn off the TV. Even though you may have a curfew from your college coaches, most of the time that only involves being in your room by a certain time. The amount of sleep you get is up to you.

The good news for student-athletes is that often their schedules are so packed with workouts, practices, classes and studying that they are sleepy a couple of hours after dinner and can sleep soundly.

There seems to be a definite connection between the amount of sleep an athlete gets and his or her performance. Cheri Mah of the Stanford Sleep Disorders Clinic and Research Laboratory has been following the sleep patterns and athletic performance of Stanford athletes for years. Her research continues to show that getting more sleep leads to better sports performance for all types of athletes.

One study she conducted followed the Stanford University women's tennis team for five weeks as they attempted to get 10 hours of sleep each night. Those who increased their sleep time ran faster sprints and hit more accurate tennis shots than those getting their usual amount of sleep.

In earlier studies, Mah found that getting extra sleep over several weeks improved performance, mood and alertness for athletes on the Stanford men's basketball team and the men's and women's swim teams.

Researchers speculate that deep sleep helps improve athletic performance because this is the time when growth hormones are released. Growth hormones stimulate muscle growth and repair, bone building and fat burning to help athletes recover.

So how much sleep do you need? Sleep experts recommend that young adults need seven to nine hours each night. Keep in mind, though, that recommendation is for regular working adults. Obviously, athletes with all their physical demands may need even more.

Here is a simple guideline for determining your optimal level of sleep. If you fall asleep within 20 minutes of going to bed and wake up without an alarm, you are probably getting the right amount of sleep. If you fall asleep immediately upon hitting the pillow and always need an alarm to wake up, you are probably sleep deprived. **Of course, don't be late for class trying your personal sleep experiment!**

Sleep is the vehicle by which we rejuvenate ourselves physically and mentally. In order to perform on the field and in the classroom, the proper amount of sleep is critical.

Here are some tips from the National Sleep Foundation for getting a great night of sleep:

- Try to go to sleep and wake up at the same time every day, even on weekends
- Avoid gadgets such as computers, tablets and phones within 60 minutes of bedtime
- Avoid caffeine and alcohol within several hours before bedtime
- Avoid drinking too many liquids before bedtime
- Cool your room at bedtime (between 60-67 degrees)

CHAMPIONSHIP POINTERS

A well spent day brings happy sleep.
Leonardo da Vinci

Better to get up late and be wide awake
than to get up early and be asleep all day.
Unknown

Early to bed and early to rise makes
a man healthy, wealthy, and wise.
Benjamin Franklin

Without enough sleep, we all become tall two-year-olds.
JoJo Jensen

CHAMPIONS DRINK RESPONSIBLY

ALCOHOL MANAGEMENT

A few years ago, singer Jamie Foxx had a hit song entitled, "Blame It." The song's subject is alcohol. Below is a sample of the song's lyrics.

Blame it on the booze
Got you feeling loose
Blame it on 'tron
Got you in the zone
Blame it on the aaaaaalcohol
Blame it on the aaaaaalcohol

Blame it on the vodka
Blame it on the Henny
Blame it on the blue top
Got you feeling dizzy
Blame it on the aaaaaalcohol
Blame it on the aaaaaalcohol

Unfortunately, in this country a lot of bad behavior is blamed on alcohol. As discussed earlier, college offers many freedoms that young people do not have in high school. College campuses are known to have great parties that often include alcohol. There are even some magazines that rank the top party schools in America. Drinking alcohol is a big challenge for young people. As a student-athlete who is known on campus, you have an even greater duty to be responsible with alcohol.

Responsible alcohol management is beneficial to student-athletes for two very important reasons. First, drinking alcohol responsibly allows you to be in the moment and remain in control of your decisions and actions. Every year there are instances of student-athletes being charged with driving under the influence, fighting in bars and sexual misconduct. Most of these occurrences relate to alcohol. People who are intoxicated make bad decisions. Often they would like to take those decisions back the next morning. Unfortunately, there is no rewind button on life.

Secondly, if an athlete chooses to drink, drinking responsibly allows them to perform optimally in their sport. According to the American Athletic Institute, here are just a few of the negative effects alcohol can have on athletes:

- **Alcohol Use Cancels Out Gains From Your Workout** – Consuming alcohol after a workout, practice, or competition can cancel out any positive gains you may have received from such activities.

- **Alcohol Use Causes Dehydration And Slows Down The Body's Ability To Heal** – Because alcohol forces use of the restroom more often, it can cause dehydration and imbalances in an athlete's system, which can lead to muscle cramps, pulls and strains.

- **Alcohol Use Prevents Muscle Recovery And Hampers Memory** – Alcohol negatively affects sleep patterns. During sleep, your muscles are able to recover and repair themselves. Interrupted sleep patterns do not allow proper muscle recovery and hamper the ability to re-member important information.

- **Alcohol Use Inhibits The Ability To Learn New Information** — One of the keys to peak athletic performance is an athlete's ability to learn new plays and strategies. When there is alcohol in an athlete's system, his or her brain is hampered in its ability to form memories. If you cannot form new memories, you cannot learn.

Dennis O'Sullivan, one of the researchers from the American Athletic Institute, also provided additional findings related to peak athletic performance.

- Drinking to intoxication can negate as much as 14 days of training effect.
- Reaction time can be affected even 12 hours after alcohol consumption.
- Athletes that drink are twice as likely to become injured.
- Alcohol compromises an athlete's already vulnerable immune system.

The negative effects of alcohol seem to present an overwhelming case for not drinking at all. However, it is likely unrealistic to believe that athletes will refrain from drinking entirely. If you choose to drink, think carefully about the effects drinking could have on your athletic and academic performance.

CHAMPIONSHIP POINTERS

✓ Never drink and drive (Have a designated driver)

✓ Be of legal age to drink

✓ Always drink in moderation

✓ Never drink within six hours of sleep

✓ Eat before you drink

✓ Alternate alcoholic drinks with non-alcoholic drinks

✓ Never mix alcohol and drugs

✓ Avoid binge drinking, such as drinking games

✓ Never leave a drink unattended

CHAMPIONS SAY NO TO DRUGS

DRUGS DESTROY DREAMS

G.O.A.T is a term used in sports to describe the Greatest of All Time. Michael Jordan is often referred to as the greatest basketball player of all time. Len Bias was often referred to as a taller, stronger version of Michael Jordan. He played for the University of Maryland. One of the major highlights of his career was scoring 35 points and handing the University of North Carolina their first ever defeat at the Dean Smith Center. On June 16, 1986, he was selected with the No. 2 pick in the NBA Draft by the Boston Celtics. Two days later, he died of a cocaine overdose. Reports indicated that he had tried cocaine for the first time to celebrate his dream of being drafted. Unfortunately, the drug killed him. He was destined to be a superstar in the NBA.

There are many types of drugs that can derail the promising career of a student-athlete. From marijuana and cocaine to Adderall and steroids, almost every type of legal and illegal drug is used by student-athletes around the country each day. The addictive effect of most drugs can cause problems long after student-athletes have finished their athletic careers. The purpose of this section is to examine briefly some of the drugs most often used by student-athletes and provide information on the potential negative effects of those drugs.

Marijuana – Marijuana goes by a variety of nicknames such as grass, Mary Jane, pot, reefer, weed, skunk, chronic or ganja. No matter what it is called, marijuana can have some very dangerous effects. There is a chemical called THC in marijuana that makes it a mind-altering substance. The amount of THC in marijuana determines its strength and effect on the user. Although marijuana is being legalized for recreational use in states around the country, it is important to note that the federal government still considers marijuana a dangerous drug and the illegal distribution and sale of marijuana is a serious crime. Below are some of the negative effects of marijuana:

Short-Term Effects of Marijuana

- Impaired judgment, perception and coordination
- Paranoia
- Hallucinations and delusions
- Rapid heart rate
- Red eyes
- Slower reaction time

Long-Term Effects of Marijuana

- Memory and learning problems

- Addiction
- Withdrawal symptoms, including weight loss, irritability and sleep problems
- Mental health problems
- Respiratory infections and bronchitis

Stimulants — As the name implies, these drugs stimulate the central nervous system. Athletes often use stimulants in an attempt to increase alertness, reduce fatigue and improve general physical performance. Many stimulants may be purchased over the counter or prescribed by a physician. Caffeine is a primary ingredient in coffee and energy drinks. Amphetamines are often contained in over-the-counter cold medicines as well. Among illegal drugs, cocaine and methamphetamine are two of the most dangerous and most often used. Below are some of the potential risks with stimulants:

- Dehydration
- Nervousness and irritability
- Insomnia
- Addiction
- Death (overdose)

There is an old saying that, "whatever goes up must come down." That is what can happen with athletes using stimulants. After a workout or game is over there is a very real possibility that an athlete will experience a "down" period. These "down" periods can have very adverse effects on athletes.

Although there are stories of athletes performing at very high levels after using drugs, there is no hard evidence to prove their use can enhance athletic performance. It is important to note that the NCAA has very strict guidelines on drug use by student-athletes. Don't risk losing games or an entire season because you were not aware of these guidelines. The best advice for athletes considering using any type of drug should be to consult a health care professional or athletic department representative first.

CHAMPIONS PLAY IT SAFE

SAFE SEX

A college president once said, "Some things never change; alumni want football, faculty want parking and students want sex." Along with all the other freedoms student-athletes have when they arrive at college, one of the most challenging things they have to deal with is being sexually responsible. In high school, most students are monitored by parents OR guardians. The ability to find the time and place for sex is tough. Both of these challenges are somewhat alleviated in college. With flexible class schedules and open visitation in most dorms, it is much easier to connect with sexual partners. There are two very real things student-athletes should be aware of related to sexual activity. First, all sexual relations should be consensual. Second, all sexual relations should be safe and free from the risk of disease or possible pregnancy.

One of the toughest concepts for young people to comprehend is sexual consent. A short definition of sexual consent is "**clear, conscious, willing and affirmative agreement to engage in sexual activity.**"

Below are the fundamental rules for consent provided by the Sexual Assault and Prevention Office at the University of South Carolina.

- A person who is incapacitated for any reason is not capable of giving consent. (A person who is drunk cannot give consent.)
- Prior consent does not guarantee future consent. (Just because there was consent last week does not mean there is consent this week.)
- The style of a person's clothing does not express consent.
- Silence or the absence of a "no" does not equal consent.
- An unconscious person cannot consent.
- Consent for one sexual act does not imply consent for other sexual acts.

- Consent can be withdrawn at any time.

All situations are different, but following these simple rules will protect students who may have any doubt about whether a sexual encounter is consensual or not. **A resource entitled "A Cup of Tea Consent Video" can be found on YouTube.**

It would be very easy to begin and end this section by just requesting that student-athletes refrain from sexual relations. Of course, that is very unrealistic. Therefore, the primary focus of this section will be to remind you of the pitfalls of unprotected sex.

As mentioned earlier, great freedom requires great responsibility. As it relates to sex, you have a responsibility to yourself, as well as to your sexual partners. As you contemplate how much you want to invest in your college athletic career, one of the things you should think strongly about is how much you are willing to sacrifice to be the best athlete that you can be. As an athlete, you are one of the most recognizable people on campus. Although you may not notice, often people are looking at you. Because of your high profile, other students might be physically attracted to you.

Most relationships start with that physical attraction. Often that physical attraction leads to sex. Great sex leads to deeper relationships. However, relationships built solely on sex will soon fizzle out. The point is, whether you are hooking up with someone for a one-night stand or you see yourself one day marrying that person, it is important that you protect yourself and the other person by using proper contraception. **Beware, no contraceptive is 100% foolproof.** There are many different types of contraceptives available for both men and women. Many will help prevent pregnancy but do not necessarily prevent contracting a sexually-transmitted disease.

CHAMPIONS TAKE CARE OF THEIR MENTAL HEALTH

A HEALTHY MIND

One of the challenges you face as a collegiate student-athlete is that you have performed at a very high level in your sport for many years. Most often you were one of the best, if not the best, player on your high school team. As such, you were counted on to make the big play when the big play needed to be made. You were the one who got the game-winning hit, made the game-winning save, hit the game-winning shot, or made the game-winning interception. Your athletic ability allowed you to be in control of those situations to a great extent.

As a collegiate student-athlete playing against better competition, you will find it much more challenging to be in control of game situations. Additionally, being away from home without your support systems will make it even more challenging. It is important to recognize that even though you are competing in sports, "**life happens.**" Things that we cannot control, like parents divorcing, grandparents passing away, illnesses of a close friend or a season-ending injury, all have the ability to affect your mental health.

Obviously, one of the primary challenges with mental health issues is that it is difficult to see what is wrong. Unlike an injury such as a broken arm or sprained ankle that provide a visual image, the mind when it is injured cannot be seen. As an athlete, when you have an injury, your coach may say something like "suck it up," "fight through the pain" or "be a man" to motivate you. Just as you would seek the advice of the team doctor or athletic trainer when you sustain an injury, it is important to understand the need to seek professional help if you are faced with mental health issues. Every college and university has specially trained counselors who will speak with you **confidentially** to help you resolve some of the challenges you may be facing. Studies have revealed that more than 30 percent of college students experience some form of depression throughout their time in college. It is unrealistic to think that there would not be a great number of student-athletes who fall into that category.

CHAMPIONS THINK BEFORE THEY POST

RESPONSIBLE SOCIAL MEDIA

One of the great things about living in America is that we enjoy the freedom of speech. We are allowed to say things that other people might deem offensive and are guaranteed that right by the First Amendment of the Constitution of the United States. It is important to note that the authors of the Constitution felt so strongly about the ability of Americans to be able to say what they want that they made freedom of speech the first amendment. However, freedom of speech does not mean freedom from consequences.

One of the biggest challenges facing student-athletes is the responsible use of social media. Sentiments that a few years ago could have been said to a few friends in a private conversation can now be broadcast literally to the entire world. Student-athletes are normally some of the most recognizable people on campus. Successful athletic teams add great value to a college or university. Fellow students, fans and alumni want to feel connected to the athletes they cheer for. Since they cannot be with those athletes in person, they choose to follow them on social media. It is important to remember that all those people who follow an athlete on social media do not always have the athlete's best interest at heart. An inappropriate post or tweet after an emotional loss can quickly be spread to other students and alumni, as well as players and fans from competing institutions and news outlets. Most college athletic departments have policies related to student-athletes on social media. Those policies range from complete freedom to coaches requiring that members of their teams not be on social media during their season. As you enter your university, make sure you are aware of the social media policies for the athletic department, as well as any that may be in place for the university's student body as a whole.

David Pertoff, a college director of athletic communications, shares these four things to keep in mind related to student-athletes' use of social media.

1. **Social Media Is A Tool, Not A Toy** – When used effectively, social media can help build a student-athlete's brand, his or her team, and his or her school.

2. **Nothing Is Truly Private...Ever** – Many student-athletes believe they can delete a tweet or their Facebook profile. Unfortunately, they do not realize that content posted on the internet can last forever.

3. **If You Retweet It (Or Share It), You Own It** – Although a student-athlete may not endorse the contents of a post, by retweeting it some of those who view it will believe they support its contents. An example of how things can go wrong is provided by Ryan Spadola. Spadola made it to the NFL as an undrafted free agent. However, as a wide receiver for Lehigh University, he retweeted an "inappropriate racial reference" before an NCAA quarterfinal game. Even though he didn't write the tweet, he was still suspended from the game.

4. **Every Tweet Reflects Who You Are** – Prospective coaches, admissions officers and future employers all use social media to learn more about candidates. What does your social media portfolio say about you?

Remember that your use of social media reflects on your personal brand. Below are a few tips to help protect your personal brand by being responsible in your use of social media:

- Don't use an inappropriate handle
- Don't get into arguments via social media
- Don't share your password with anyone
- Don't post negative statements about teammates, coaches or your competition
- Never use inappropriate language
- Never post inappropriate photos
- Never post anything immediately following a loss

- Never post anything when you should be asleep
- Do post words of thanks to fans, teammates, alumni and family
- Do use correct grammar and spelling
- Do recognize the accomplishments of others
- Do share positive information about your interests and hobbies
- Do share motivational and inspirational information
- Do share good deeds about your school and your community

Probably some of the best advice on student-athletes using social media responsibly comes from the professional football player and future Hall of Famer, J.J. Watt. "Read each tweet about 95 times before you send it. Look at every Instagram post about 95 times before you send it. A reputation takes years and years and years to build and it takes one press of a button to ruin it. Don't let that happen to you. You've done so much work, you've put in so much effort. Don't let one moment ruin your entire life because you wanted to be funny or you were mad or because you had a mood."

CHAMPIONS TAKE CARE
OF THEIR MONEY

FINANCIAL FITNESS

The thought of paying for six pizzas three years after they were eaten sounds pretty ridiculous. Students who are not wise with their finances could easily face this scenario. Credit card companies often offer free merchandise for students to sign up for credit cards. Not realizing that credit cards do not equal free money, they begin using the cards for perishable items like pizza. Months after the pizza has been consumed by others in the dorm they are still paying on the $125 bill. Similarly, items that do not significantly contribute to your education like an orange pair of shoes that can only be worn once during the semester are not wise purchases. Student-athletes receive money in many different ways. Some at the highest level will receive a cost of attendance check each month. Others will receive money from financial aid. Still others will receive a certain amount of money from home each month. The responsibility is the same no matter how much you receive. You must be wise with your finances. The same discipline you have used to become an elite athlete must be used to control spending. Discipline often means sacrifice. There will be some things you must sacrifice that you may want but not need in order to maintain a healthy bank account.

Below is an example of how credit card companies make their money. This example shows that if the credit card company is owed $1,500, it will take 51 months (4 years and 3 months) to pay off the balance if the minimum monthly payment of $40 is paid each month.

Credit Card Balance	$1,500
APR (Annual Percentage Rate) Interest	14%
Minimum Monthly Payment	$40
Total Time To Pay Off Balance	51 months
Total Interest Paid	$521
Total Paid (Balance Plus Interest)	$2,021

Here are some tips to manage your finances successfully:

- Develop a monthly budget
- Separate wants from needs
- Set up a checking account
- Use coupons when possible

CHAMPIONS CONNECT
WITH A MENTOR

MENTORS MAKE THE DIFFERENCE

Imagine that you and your best friend were traveling from Charlotte, North Carolina, to Washington, D.C. Unfortunately, you could not travel together and both would be driving separate automobiles. Upon arriving, your friend asks how your trip went. You say it was uneventful except you got a speeding ticket right outside of Richmond, Virginia.

Imagine your disappointment when your friend shares that he received a ticket at the same spot earlier that day. You would immediately ask why he did not call you to warn you about the officer at that location.

One of the most valuable assets you can have as a new student-athlete is a mentor. Mentors provide that call back that allows you to slow down and not get the speeding ticket. Mentors, in many cases, have made some of the mistakes you are bound to make if you don't get good advice. It is important upon arriving on campus that you find a mentor who can help you navigate your time in college. Mentors come in various forms. It can be an upperclassman on your team or an older student-athlete from another team. It can be a coach, athletic trainer, equipment manager or other athletic department staff member. It can even be one of your professors with whom you develop a close relationship. The most important thing is that you find someone who can share his or her wisdom and advice and hold you accountable as a student-athlete. Often these relationships last long after your collegiate playing days.

It is often said that you can't have success without a successor. As you benefit from the relationship that you build with your mentor, it is important to understand your role as a mentor to younger student-athletes.

CHAMPIONS ASSOCIATE
WITH GREAT FRIENDS

FINDING TRUE FRIENDS

One of the most brilliant marketing strategies that Facebook employed in its start-up process was to encourage people to become friends on Facebook. As a result, the term "friend" has been diminished over the years. Student-athletes need to recognize the difference between friends and associates. A true friend is someone who always has your best interests at heart. They hold you accountable. They make you better. They keep you out of situations they know could be a problem. In your life, you will be very fortunate if you have five true friends. All other people you are acquainted with should just be considered associates. Associates may care about your success, but often that motivation is connected to their desire to be associated with you because of your success. As you begin your college career as a student-athlete, be very careful who you allow into your inner circle. Make sure before you call someone a friend that they truly are your friend.

CHAMPIONSHIP POINTERS

To be a winner you must associate with winners.
Dexter Yager

Show me a person's friends and I will show you his future.
Ronnie Melancon

One bad apple can spoil the whole bunch.
Grandma

CHAMPIONS RESPECT ALL PEOPLE

EMBRACING DIVERSITY

Diversity is a word often used in this country. It speaks to the differences between people. Very often, the term diversity has come to be a discussion about race and more specifically about black versus white. It is very important to note that diversity encompasses many things other than race. **These other dimensions include: age, gender, national origin, sexual orientation, veteran status, religion, sex, disability and genetics**.

One of the most exciting things about attending college is all the new people you meet. College campuses are among the most diverse environments in the world. As a student-athlete, you have several advantages over your fellow students. One of those advantages is that you have a built-in social circle in your teammates. More than likely, your team will be made up of a very diverse group of individuals. As you compete with your teammates, you will undoubtedly get to know them on a very personal level. One disadvantage is that because you have this built-in social circle you may not be forced to move out of your comfort zone and seek out new and diverse relationships.

People will be attracted to you and want to get to know you because you play a sport. Like it or not, you will be one of the most recognizable people on your campus. Ask students the name of the student body president and perhaps 20 percent will know their name. Ask the same group of students the name of the starting quarterback on the football team and it is likely over 80 percent will know his name.

One of the great opportunities for you as a student-athlete is to get to know your fellow students on a personal level. Taking time before or after class to get to know the student seated next to you is a great way to expand your circle. Even if you are shy, all you have to do is ask someone to tell you a little about themselves. One thing people love to do is talk about themselves. That simple request to find out more about someone will naturally lead to other questions like why did you choose this university or what is your dream job?

CHAMPIONSHIP POINTERS

Never judge a book by its cover.
American Wisdom

Variety is the spice of life.
American Proverb

Diversity is the one true thing we all have in common.
Unknown

It is the difference of opinion that makes horse races.
Mark Twain

CHAMPIONS EAT THE RIGHT WAY

DINING ETIQUETTE

Many years ago at a conference, I heard a college coach speak about one of his players that was to receive a national award. The coach and player were staying at a very fancy hotel, at which the banquet was also being held. When the player went downstairs that afternoon before the evening banquet, he was so intimidated by the place settings on the table that he left the hotel and went to the nearest McDonald's to eat. He was not familiar with all the forks, knives, spoons, glasses and plates. Just like that young man, most of us only need a fork and maybe a knife when we eat at home. Just like that young man, we may also have to attend a special lunch or dinner one day. The good news is we don't have to be intimidated or scared when we see a lot of forks, knives, spoons, glasses and plates on a table. Below is a simple place setting diagram. Following the diagram are a few very simple rules for dining etiquette.

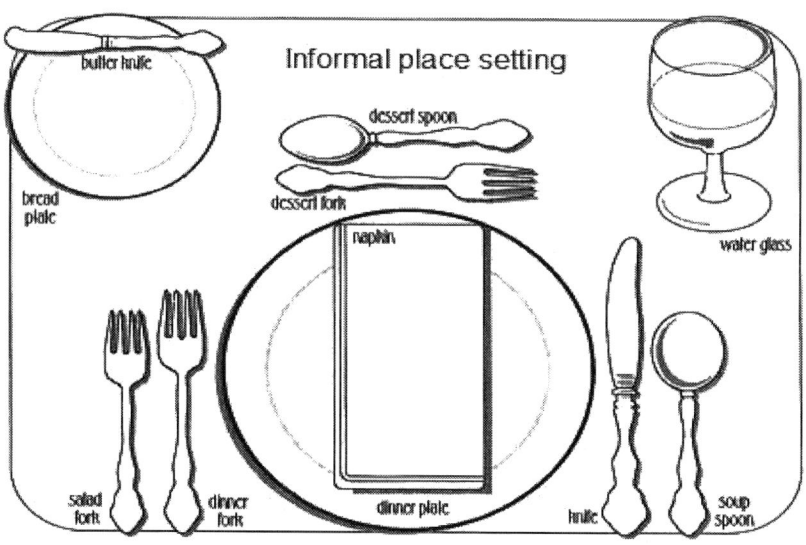

Here are some simple rules for dining etiquette and table manners:

- Allow adults to be seated first.
- Always chew with your mouth closed.
- Do not talk with your mouth full.
- Cut your food and take small manageable bites.
- Place your napkin in your lap.
- If you must leave the table, be sure to excuse yourself.
- Wait until after you have tasted your food before adding salt or pepper.
- Salt and pepper are always passed together. Even if only one is requested.
- Always pass items to your right.
- Never place your elbows on the table.
- Start your meal with the utensils (forks, spoons) on the outside of your place setting first.
- Bread plates are on the left and water is on the right. (Remember BMW: Bread-Meal-Water)

CHAMPIONS KNOW THE RULES

NCAA COMPLIANCE

Earlier in this book, the subject of academic integrity was discussed. Just as it is important to play by the rules academically, it is also important to play by the rules as it relates to athletics. The National Collegiate Athletic Association is the governing body for collegiate athletics. One of the primary goals of the NCAA is to create a level playing field. Theoretically, if everyone is playing by the same rules off the field, the best teams will win the games on the field.

They have guidelines and rules for everything from how many hours a week a student-athlete may practice to the substances that are legal in your body during competition. Most of the larger universities in this country have an assistant athletic director who is responsible for compliance. Smaller colleges and universities might have an athletic staff member who has compliance duties among their other responsibilities. It is important for student-athletes to understand that even though they have the athletic department compliance staff as a resource, the ultimate responsibility for not breaking rules rests with themselves. Just like getting a speeding ticket and telling the officer you didn't realize you were in a school zone, committing a rules infraction and saying you didn't even know it existed is not a defense.

There will be consequences for rules you break. These consequences could range from reprimands for smaller offenses to a whole program being given the "Death Penalty" for continual major infractions. Your coaches cannot know all of the compliance rules and regulations. Therefore, you must seek to learn the rules that apply to you as a student-athlete. Most athletic departments have these rules posted on their website or they can be accessed through the NCAA offices. Take time to read those rules and ask questions of the athletic department representative who is responsible for athletic compliance.

CHAMPIONS FIND ROOM FOR IMPROVEMENT

GETTING BETTER EVERY DAY

Question: What is the biggest room in the house?
Answer: The biggest room in the house is the room for improvement.

Over the years as I have watched great athletes conduct interviews after sporting events, one thing that I have found they all have in common is a desire to get better. Rarely, even after winning a championship, will you hear a great athlete say that he or she has reached the peak levels of their performance. Whether he or she has won or lost, at some point during the interview the athlete will say he or she is going to go back and look at the film and find a way to get better.

I have developed a contract that is designed to be signed by you and an accountability partner. The concept behind this contract is that at the end of each day, you will self-evaluate and ask yourself one simple question: **"Did I get better today?"**

I encourage you to think thoughtfully about this contract. Find an accountability partner that will make sure that you are doing something each day to get better. Imagine the cumulative effect of small changes each day that produce a better you. As you get better, the team will get better. Whether it's doing one extra set of sit-ups, learning a new word or having a conversation with an international student, there are many different ways you can get better. Below is the **Better Contract.**

BETTER ATHLETE CONTRACT

I _____ understand I have
not reached my full potential as an athlete. I know that in order to reach my
full potential I must get BETTER! I hereby pledge that I will make an effort
every day to get BETTER. I understand that:

- Greatness never takes a day off!
- Hard work will always beat talent when talent refuses to work hard!
- My toughest opponent will always be the mirror!
- Actions have consequences; I will be responsible for my actions!
- In adversity, I will always find opportunity!
- Past success does not guarantee future results!
- When I get better, the team gets better!
- I will always train for double overtime!
- Respect is earned, not given!
- No excuses – just results!

At the end of each day, the one and only question I need to ask myself is,
"Did I get BETTER today?" I Will Get BETTER!

Signed_____ Date_____

Witness _____Date_____

WORK CITED

"Guide to Choosing College Majors." The Princeton Review.

University of South Carolina. **A Student Guide to the Honor Code**. Columbia, South Carolina.

Jaret, Peter. **"5 Nutrition Tips for Athletes."** WebMD.

Newsroom, Alec Rosenberg UC. **"How to Sleep like a Pro (athlete)."** University of California.

O'Sullivan, Dennis. **"Alcohol & Athletic Performance."** American Athletic Institute.

Gaio, Michael. **"Social Media Dos and Don'ts for Student-Athletes."** Athletic Business.

University of South Carolina. **"Sexual Assault Awareness and Prevention."** Columbia, South Carolina.

"Stimulants." World of Sports Science.

"Performance-Enhancing Drugs: Know the Risks." Mayo Clinic. Mayo Foundation for Medical Education and Research.

"Effects of Using Drugs." The Coach's Playbook Against Drugs.

"What Kind of Drug Counts as Marijuana?" New Health Advisor.

OTHER PRODUCTS BY
Adonis "Sporty" Jeralds

The Champion In You
The first book by Adonis "Sporty" Jeralds. This simple book reveals the secrets of success. Like "Let Your Light Shine," this book is a collection of short vignettes that focus on integrity, community service, goal setting, excellence and hard work. A classic!

Let Your Light Shine
The second book by Adonis "Sporty" Jeralds. This book reveals additional secrets of success. Like "The Champion In You, this book is a collection of short vignettes that focus on courage, talent development, integrity, and personal responsibility.

Follow The Bouncing Ball
This short story follows four employees of the Big Time Coliseum and how they deal with their major league team leaving. This "quick read" will help individuals understand the need to embrace the change we all are experiencing in our organizations.

The Champion's Club—Male Edition
This workbook is designed as a character education based tool. It is designed to be used by a select group of young men in a school, after school program, church or other organization. This product is an excellent tool to engage mentors as it provides a blueprint from which to work with young men.

The Champion's Club—Female Edition—
Co-Authored With Jazmine Jeralds
This workbook is designed as a character education based tool. It is designed to be used by a select group of young women in a school, after school program, church or other organization. This product is an excellent tool to engage mentors as it provides a blueprint from which to work with young women.

To order additional products or to book a presentation, please contact:

Adonis "Sporty" Jeralds
E-Mail: adonis.jeralds@gmail.com
Phone: 980 721-2515

PRESENTATIONS BY
Adonis "Sporty" Jeralds

FROM THE LOCKEROOM TO THE CLASS ROOM
Based on the book, this interactive workshop is designed for freshmen student athletes. Using information from over 25 years of teaching at the collegiate level this presentation will help student athletes understand the challenges of moving from high school to the collegiate level.

LET YOUR LIGHT SHINE
Based on the hugely popular book, Let Your Light Shine, this keynote speech or seminar is designed to empower individuals to believe, achieve and realize that everyone can live their dreams. Everyone can SHINE.

CHAMPION
A motivational seminar designed for individuals seeking greater fulfillment in their lives. Developed from the book, The Champion In You, this presentation reveals the secret to attaining success while maintaining personal satisfaction.

FOLLOW THE BOUNCING BALL
This inter-active presentation based on the popular book, Follow The Bouncing Ball, focuses on how individuals and organizations deal with change. This presentation is designed for the entire organization—from the CEO to the mail room attendant. This presentation will benefit organizations going through re-organization, downsizing or growth in the market place.

MISSION POSSIBLE
A two-part interactive seminar created for individuals who want to take control of their lives through the development of goals and the creation of personal mission statements.

For more information, to order additional copies or to book a presentation, please contact:

Adonis "Sporty" Jeralds
E-Mail: adonis.jeralds@gmail.com
Phone: 980 721-2515

ABOUT THE AUTHOR

Adonis "Sporty" Jeralds is a professor, businessman, consultant, speaker and author. He holds an undergraduate degree from Guilford College and two master's degrees, in public administration and sport management, from UNC Chapel Hill and the University of Massachusetts. He was manager of the Charlotte Coliseum for 15 years. In his career he coordinated such internationally recognized events as the Men's and Women's Final Four, The ACC Tournament, The NBA All-Star Game, and visits from the Rolling Stones and Mother Teresa. He is a full-time instructor at the University of South Carolina and works as a community advisor with the Charlotte Hornets.

He is the author of three other highly successful books, *The Champion In You*, *Let Your Light Shine*, and *Follow The Bouncing Ball*. His speaking engagements have inspired audiences around the world. He resides in Charlotte, North Carolina. He and his wife Teresa are the proud parents of Jazmine and Jacob.

NOTES

NOTES

NOTES